THE FRIESIAN HORSE

By Sara Green

Consultant:
Dr. Emily Leuthner
DVM, MS, DACVIM
Country View Veterinary Service
Oregon, Wisc.

BELLWETHER MEDIA • MINNEAPOLIS, MN

Jump into the cockpit and take flight
with Pilot Books. Your journey will
take you on high-energy adventures
as you learn about all that is wild,
weird, fascinating, and fun!

This edition first published in 2012 by Bellwether Media, Inc.

No part of this publication may be reproduced in whole or in part without written permission of the publisher.
For information regarding permission, write to Bellwether Media, Inc., Attention: Permissions Department,
5357 Penn Avenue South, Minneapolis, MN 55419.

Library of Congress Cataloging-in-Publication Data

Green, Sara, 1964-
 The Friesian horse / by Sara Green.
    p. cm. – (Pilot books. Horse breed roundup)
 Includes bibliographical references and index.
 Summary: "Engaging images accompany information about the Friesian Horse. The combination of high-interest subject
matter and narrative text is intended for students in grades 3 through 7"–Provided by publisher.
 ISBN 978-1-60014-737-1 (hardcover : alk. paper)
 1. Friesian horse–Juvenile literature. I. Title.
 SF293.F9G74 2012
 636.1'3–dc23   2011029089

Printed in the United States of America, North Mankato, MN.

010112   1204

CONTENTS

The Friesian Horse

The crowd awaits the arrival of the magnificent Friesians into the **show ring**. People have come a long way to see this rare breed up close. Two jet-black Friesians come into view. They are wearing harnesses and pulling an elaborate carriage driven by a man in a top hat. All eyes are on the noble horses as they move briskly around the ring. They are a spectacular sight!

Many people consider Friesians to be one of the most beautiful horse breeds in the world. With their striking black coats, flowing manes, and long tails, the elegant horses are always an impressive sight. The breed is also known for its calm, friendly **temperament**. Horse lovers around the world admire the good looks and gentle nature of the Friesian.

Friesians are large **draft horses** that usually weigh between 1,300 and 1,600 pounds (590 and 730 kilograms). They stand 14 to 17 **hands** high at the **withers**. This is 4.6 to 5.6 feet (1.4 to 1.7 meters) tall.

Friesians are easy to recognize. Almost all **purebred** Friesians are entirely black. Some have a small white marking called a star on their foreheads. Older Friesians appear brown in color because their black coats lighten after years of being in the sun. Friesians have long and elegant heads and necks. The tips of their small, alert ears bend slightly inward. They have strong, muscular bodies and powerful **hindquarters**. Their steps are high and springy. Friesians have long hair called feather on the back of their lower legs. Their manes and tails are long, thick, and wavy. Some manes and tails grow so long that they touch the ground!

Fit for a Queen

Queen Beatrix of the Netherlands keeps a stable of Friesians. On the first day the Dutch parliament meets every year, a team of eight Friesians pulls Queen Beatrix in a golden coach to the parliament buildings.

Warhorses, Workhorses, and the Studbook Society

The Friesian is one of the oldest **domesticated** horse breeds in Europe. It came from a region of the Netherlands called Friesland around 2,500 years ago. The people of Friesland bred large, heavy draft horses. During the **Middle Ages**, heavily armored Dutch and German knights rode these strong horses into battle. They called them Friesians. For centuries, Friesians were considered the best warhorses in Europe.

Over time, people stopped using Friesians as warhorses. Instead, Friesians worked on farms, pulled people in carriages, and were used as riding horses. During the 1500s, breeders **crossbred** Friesians with Spanish Andalusian horses. The result was a slimmer, more elegant horse with a smaller head, longer neck, and a high, springy step. This horse became known as the Modern Friesian. People also continued to breed the larger, heavier Friesian. This type became known as the Baroque Friesian. Both types are still bred today.

The popularity of Friesians dropped during the 1800s. Farmers chose larger, heavier draft horses to plow their fields. Few people were still breeding Friesians. By the late 1800s, only a few Friesian **stallions** remained in the world. In 1879, a group of Friesian owners in the Netherlands decided to save the breed. Using strict guidelines, the owners continued to breed their Friesians. They started the Studbook Society to **register** purebred Friesians and horses that were part Friesian.

In the 1970s, breeders Thomas Hannon and Frank Leyendekker brought Friesians to the United States. In 1983, Leyendekker helped start a new branch of the Studbook Society called the Friesian Horse Association of North America (FHANA). This group keeps track of all Friesians born in North America or brought to North America from Europe. Today, about 40,000 Friesians are registered worldwide with the Studbook Society. About 7,000 of these are also members of the FHANA.

The Black Pearl

The Friesian is the only horse breed native to the Netherlands. It is often called "The Black Pearl of Friesland."

The Studbook Society has strict rules about which Friesians are allowed to have **foals**. Only the best horses are approved to breed. All Friesians must participate in a judging event called a **keuring**. Judges from the Studbook Society fly all over the world to review each horse. Friesians go through two rounds of judging. The first takes place when they are foals. The judges come again when Friesians are around three years old.

Judges give the horses grades for their appearance and movement. The best **mares** are given a rating of *ster*, the Dutch word for "star." Mares with *ster* ratings often become mothers. The Studbook Society also decides which stallions are allowed to breed. Only the top stallions are selected. Today, fewer than 35 Friesian stallions are approved to breed in the United States.

Name that Friesian

Each year the Studbook Society picks several letters of the alphabet for naming purposes. The names of all Friesian foals registered that year have to begin with one of these letters. For example, the names of foals born in 2012 must begin with M, N, or O.

Elegance in the Show Ring

Today's Friesian is known for its beauty and skill in the show ring. Imagine attending a horse show with hundreds of elegant black Friesians! The International Friesian Show Horse Association (IFSHA) sponsors national and international shows that feature a variety of events. One of the crowd's favorites is the pleasure driving competition. Friesians are **hitched** to carts that have two or four wheels. The horses pull the carts at different **gaits**. Judges award points to the horses for their behavior, performance, and appearance.

In some competitions, Friesians pull a carriage called a *sjee*. People used this type of carriage long ago in Friesland. A *sjee* has two large wheels and elaborate designs. In competitions, drivers and passengers wear traditional 1860s clothing from Friesland. Judges award points for the presentation of the *sjee*, the costumes, and the performance of the horses.

Another popular IFSHA event is **dressage**. In dressage, riders guide their horses through a variety of movements. They begin by performing gaits and turns. Advanced horses perform **choreographed** movements set to music. With their shiny black coats, flowing manes, and long tails, the Friesians make a great impression on both the judges and the audience.

Friesians also entertain audiences in other ways. If you have been to the circus, you may have seen a Friesian in the show ring. Friesians are popular circus horses. They can perform many difficult tricks. Some have been trained to walk on their back legs, carry acrobats doing stunts, and take a bow!

Famous Friesians

Paulus 121

Paulus 121 was a stallion born in 1913. At the time, only three Friesian stallions in the world were approved to breed. The breed was in danger of extinction. In 1916, the FHANA purchased Paulus 121 and gave him a premium title. This title allowed him to breed. He fathered so many foals that he became one of the breed's foundation stallions. Today, most Friesians can trace their bloodlines to him.

Othello

Othello was a Friesian that portrayed the horse Goliath in the 1985 film *Ladyhawke*. Othello's performance gave many viewers their first glimpse of a Friesian. He helped increase the breed's popularity around the world. Before being cast in the film, Othello performed in a circus for trick rider Manuela Beeloo. Othello retired in 1994.

Nanning 374

Nanning 374 was a stallion that lived in Wisconsin. Born in 1996, Nanning 374 was known for his remarkable bloodlines and beauty. He won the Champion ribbon at the 2002 Stallion Inspection in the Netherlands. He was also famous for producing excellent foals. Nanning 374 died in 2010.

The Friesian breed has been close to **extinction** a few times. However, someone has always stepped in to save the breed. Today, the Friesian population continues to grow. Most Friesians live in the Netherlands and Germany. Their numbers are also steadily increasing in North America, especially in the United States.

Their beauty is only part of what makes Friesians so captivating. Friesians are also intelligent and athletic. These qualities have helped them become more popular. Above all, Friesians are gentle, friendly companions and riding horses. They form strong bonds with people of all ages. People who own Friesians know just how unique their horses are. Many would not dream of owning any other breed. It's clear that the magnificent Friesians are here to stay!

Glossary

choreographed—having a planned sequence of steps and moves

crossbred—used two different breeds of an animal to produce a new breed

domesticated—tamed; domesticated animals are used to living near people.

draft horses—large, tall horses used for heavy physical labor

dressage—a specific kind of horse training; dressage horses perform movements like spins and turns at the command of their riders.

extinction—when every member of a species or breed has died

foals—young horses; foals are under one year old.

gaits—the ways in which a horse moves; walking, trotting, and cantering are examples of gaits.

hands—the units used to measure the height of a horse; one hand is equal to 4 inches (10.2 centimeters).

hindquarters—the hind legs and muscles of a four-legged animal

hitched—attached to a carriage or wagon with harnesses and chains

keuring—an event where judges evaluate Friesian horses on appearance and movement

mares—adult female horses

Middle Ages—a period in Europe that lasted from the 500s to the 1500s

purebred—born from parents of the same breed

register—to make record of; owners register their horses with official breed organizations.

show ring—the ring where horses compete and are displayed at a horse show

stallions—adult male horses that are used for breeding

temperament—personality or nature; the Friesian has a calm, friendly temperament.

withers—the ridge between the shoulder blades of a horse

At the Library

Beeman, Laura. *The Friesian Horse*. West Conshohocken, Pa.: Infinity Publishing, 2001.

Coleman, Lori. *The Friesian Horse*. Mankato, Minn.: Capstone Press, 2006.

Littlefield, Cindy A. *Horse Games & Puzzles for Kids: 102 Brainteasers, Word Games, Jokes & Riddles, Picture Puzzles, Matches & Logic Tests for Horse-Loving Kids.* North Adams, Mass.: Storey Publishing, 2004.

On the Web

Learning more about Friesians is as easy as 1, 2, 3.

1. Go to www.factsurfer.com.

2. Enter "Friesians" into the search box.

3. Click the "Surf" button and you will see a list of related Web sites.

With factsurfer.com, finding more information is just a click away.

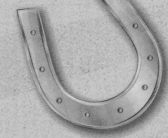

The images in this book are reproduced through the courtesy of: Zuzule, front cover; katewarn images / Alamy, pp. 4-5; Lenkaden, pp. 6-7; Abramova Kseniya, p. 8; Only Horses Tbk / Alamy, p. 9; Sabine Stuewer / KimballStock, pp. 10-11; Sarah K. Andrew, pp. 12-13; Carol Walker / Minden Pictures, pp. 14-15; Dennis Donohue, pp. 16-17; Juniors Bildarchiv / Alamy, pp. 18-19; Manfred Grebler / Alamy, pp. 20-21.